THE HAMPSHIRE
COLOURING BOOK

First published 2016
Reprinted 2017, 2019

The History Press
97 St George's Place,
Cheltenham GL50 3QB
www.thehistorypress.co.uk

British Library Cataloguing in Publication Data.
A catalogue record for this book is available from the British Library.

ISBN 978 0 7509 6804 1

Cover colouring by Lucy Hester.
Typesetting and origination by The History Press
Printed in Turkey by Imak.

THE HAMPSHIRE
COLOURING BOOK

PAST AND PRESENT

Take some time out of your busy life to relax and unwind with this feel-good colouring book designed for everyone who loves Hampshire.

Absorb yourself in the simple action of colouring in the scenes and settings from around the county of Hampshire, past and present. From iconic architecture to picturesque coastal vistas, you are sure to find some of your favourite locations waiting to be transformed with a splash of colour. Bring these scenes alive as you de-stress with this inspiring and calming colouring book.

There are no rules – choose any page and any choice of colouring pens or pencils you like to create your own unique, colourful and creative illustrations.

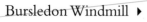

Bursledon Windmill ▸

Jane Austen's House Museum, Alton ▸

Hayling Island beach ▸

A wartime mobile kitchen set up beside the
ruins of Holyrood church in Southampton for
the police and local military personnel ▸

An alpaca at Hensting, Eastleigh ▶

Milestones Museum of
Living History, Basingstoke ▸

Netley Abbey ▶

Breamore House and Countryside
Museum, near Fordingbridge ▸

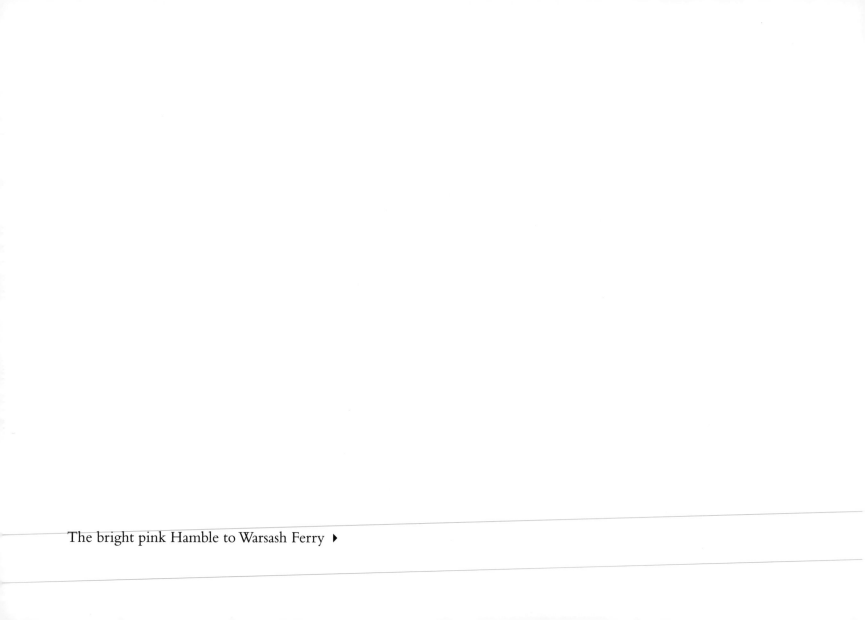

The bright pink Hamble to Warsash Ferry ▸

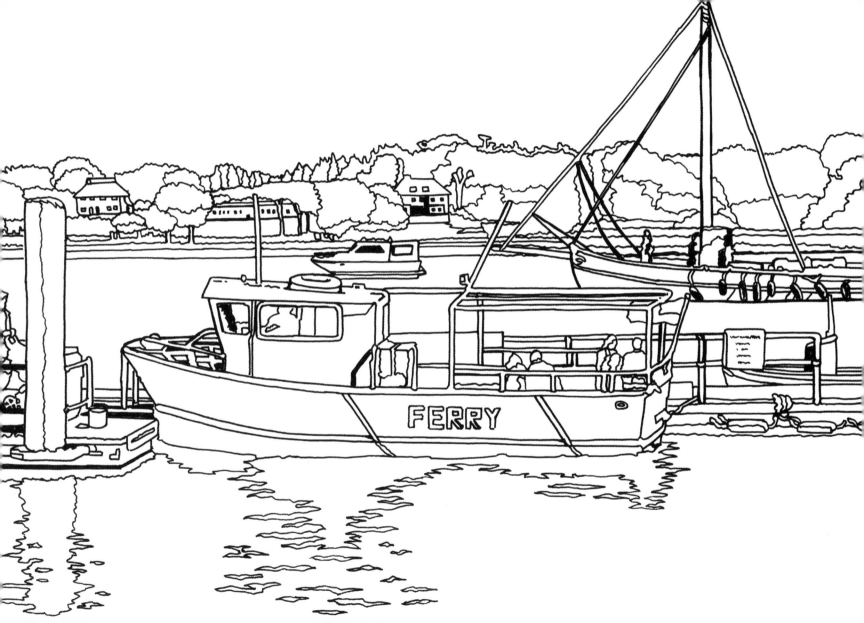

Portsmouth Cathedral ▶

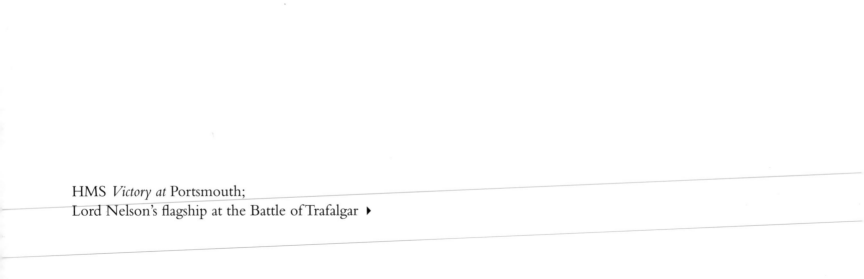

HMS *Victory at* Portsmouth;
Lord Nelson's flagship at the Battle of Trafalgar ▸

Portsmouth City Museum ▸

New Forest Wildlife Park, near Ashurst ▸

Winchester Cathedral ▶

Wolvesey Castle, Winchester ▶

The Spinnaker Tower,
Gunwharf Quays, Portsmouth ▸

Avington Park, Winchester ▶

Portchester Castle ▶

Lee-on-the-Solent beach ▶

The Mary Rose Museum, Portsmouth ▸

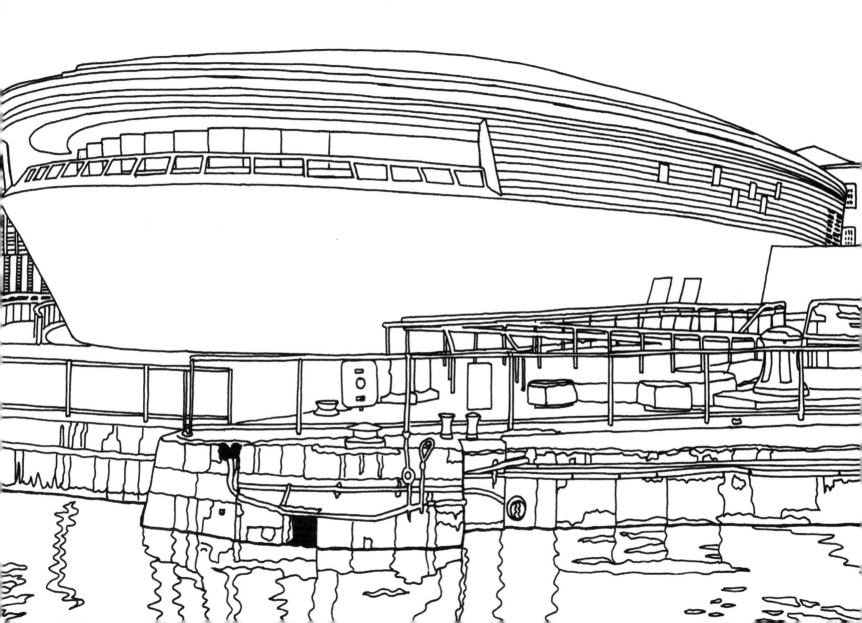

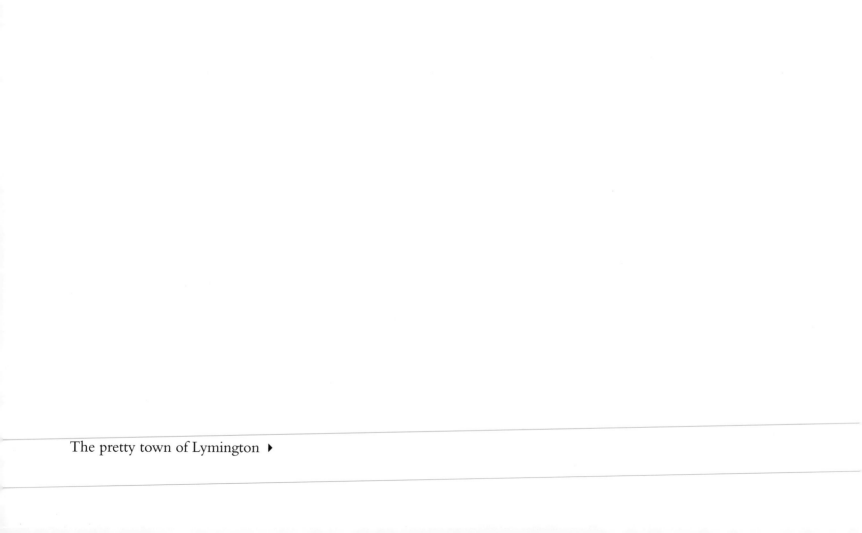

The pretty town of Lymington ▶

A hydrofoil passenger ferry crosses the Solent
between Hampshire and the Isle of Wight ▸

HMS *Warrior*, Portsmouth Naval Base ▶

Winchester Castle ▶

Bridge over the River Itchen
and Winchester City Mill ▸

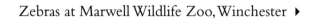

Zebras at Marwell Wildlife Zoo, Winchester ▶

Tudor House and Garden, Southampton ▸

Gosport Ferry ▸

Southsea Castle with its dry moat in the foreground ▸

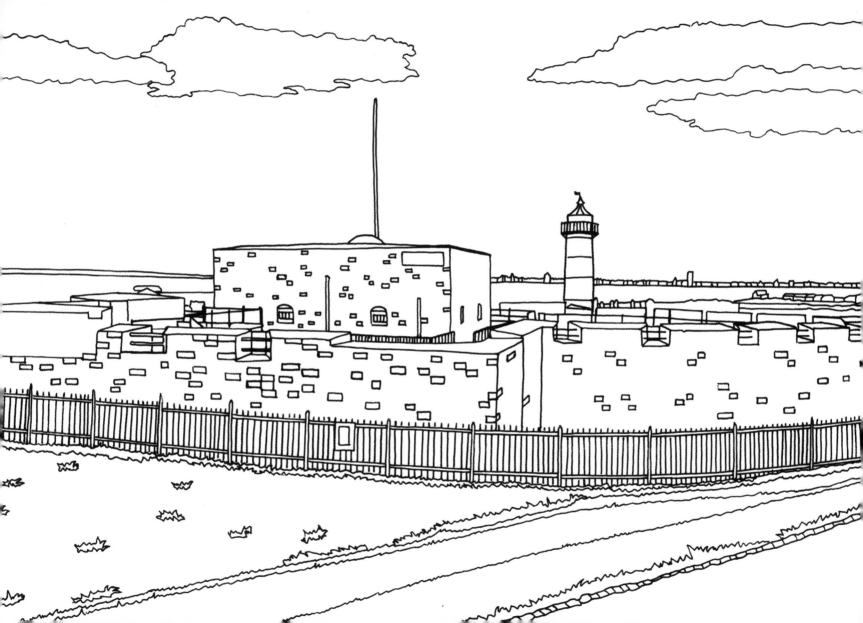

Titchfield Abbey ▸

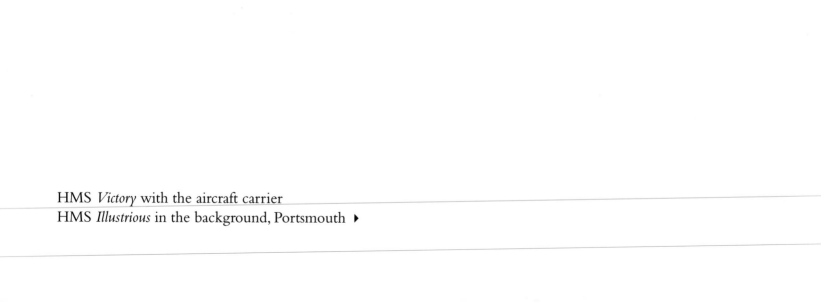

HMS *Victory* with the aircraft carrier
HMS *Illustrious* in the background, Portsmouth ▸

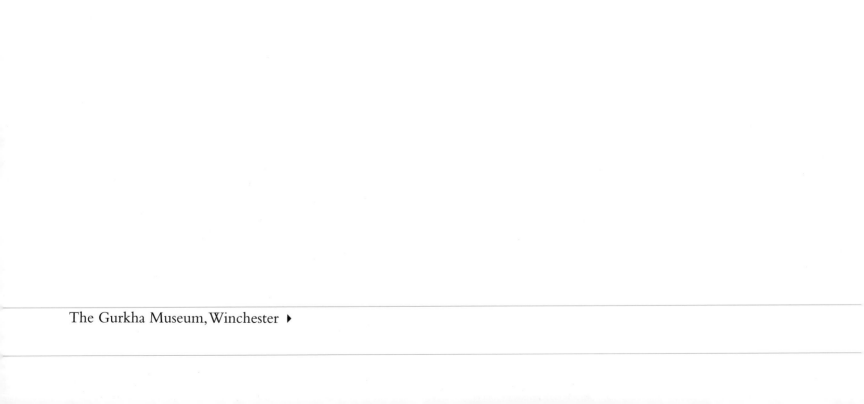

The Gurkha Museum, Winchester ▸

Isle of Wight hovercraft ▸

Romsey Abbey ▸

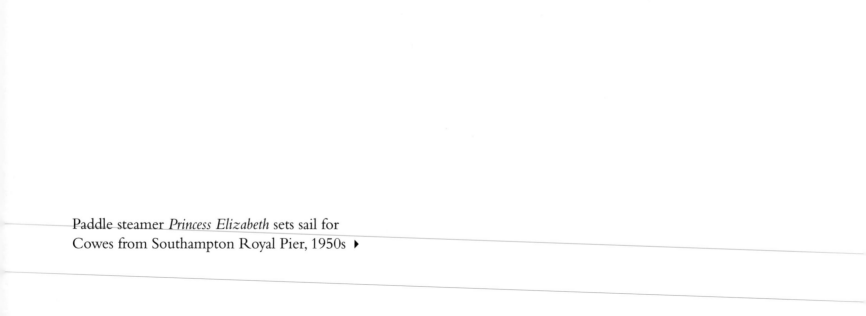

Paddle steamer *Princess Elizabeth* sets sail for
Cowes from Southampton Royal Pier, 1950s ▶

The Bargate, Southampton, in 1910 ▸

South Parade Pier, Portsmouth, *c.* 1909 ▸

Two New Forest ponies ▶

Whitchurch Silk Mill ▶

HMS *Alliance* submarine at Gosport ▶

Charles Dickens's birthplace on
Old Commercial Road, Portsmouth ▶

Mid Hants Railway, Alton Station ▸